CAMPFIRE STORIES

Volume 12

Tales of the Wild West Series

5-5-1994

Rick Steber

Illustrations by Don Gray

NOTE
Campfire Stories is the twelfth book in the
Tales of the Wild West Series

Campfire Stories
Volume 12
Tales of the Wild West Series

Bonanza Publishing
Box 204
Prineville, Oregon 97754

INTRODUCTION

The storyteller spins a web of fantasy while the campfire sends a shower of sparks leaping into the night sky to drift among the ancient stars. It is in this manner that the history of mankind has been passed from one generation to the next.

In North America the native people formed their cultures and spiritual beliefs through stories. Stories described the origins of earth and mankind, of floods, fires, hunts, wars, heros, the supernatural, myths and legends. Young people knew what had happened in the world because their elders communicated it to them around the campfire.

The first Europeans to make their way among the Indians were mountain men who told fantastic and mystifying tales of great cities to the east and other worlds that existed across the great shiny waters. Each successive wave of white invaders brought with it a different blend of fact and fiction.

In today's world it might appear that campfire stories can no longer compete with movies and television. But no special effect can ever come close to the power and impact of human imagination.

Try reading or telling a story around the campfire. Watch the faces of your listeners and know the value and significance of keeping alive our time-honored traditions of oral history.

GIANT

The Coquille Indians of the southern Oregon coast have passed the story of the cannibal giant from generation to generation. The story teller relates: "One day a giant appeared. From where did he come? From the deep woods to the east? From the sky above? Or did he crawl up from the depths of the sea?

"This creature was hairy, had long arms and legs and strong muscles. Proportionally his head was much too large for his body and this gave him a hateful, hideous look.

"The Indians were curious. They came to stare at him, but were afraid to get too close, afraid he might harm them. And so they watched from a safe distance.

"The giant took refuge in a cave. He could often be observed sitting near the entrance of his cave or walking in the hard-packed sand along the beach.

"When the first child vanished it was assumed a wave had washed him away. But then a second and third child disappeared and the Indians began to wonder if the giant in the cave did not have something to do with the disappearances.

"'I have never seen the giant eat,' testified one of the men.

"'Then we shall watch the giant, day and night. We will discover what he eats.'

"The second day the guard posted near the entrance to the cave listened to the giant call to a group of Indian children, asking them to help him gather shells. He promised them food and special trinkets. One boy came near. When he was within reach the giant grabbed him, wrapped him in his blanket and carried him off to his cave.

"Although the Indians could not save the boy they were able to devise a plan. They waited until the giant had eaten his fill and had fallen asleep. Then they plugged the entrance to the cave with boulders and dropped hot ashes and wood down the smoke hole. Fire consumed the flesh-eating giant."

IKTOMI AND THE DUCKS

Iktomi was a shadowy spirit of the world beyond. And while he could perform great acts of bravery he could also be a coward and a very evil spirit.

One time Iktomi, who had not a single friend and no one who really loved him, was walking along a path beside the lake, carrying a blanket with the corners tied.

A flock of ducks called to him, "Stop! Show us what you have in your blanket! We must know," the ducks shouted in unison. They crowded around him and some even brushed their wings against the mysterious bundle.

Iktomi carefully set his blanket on the ground. He told the ducks, "It is only a pack of songs that I bring along with me."

"They must be wonderful. Allow us to hear these songs," called the ducks.

At length Iktomi consented but said, "I never sing my songs in the open air. Go quickly, gather leaves and grass for me."

Iktomi went to work cutting willow sticks. These he bent and pushed the ends into the ground, making a framework. He had the ducks cover this with materials. Soon the hut was completed and Iktomi stepped inside, seated himself and invited the ducks to join him.

Iktomi instructed the ducks to close their eyes and dance. He warned them, saying if they opened their eyes they would forever after have red eyes. In a strange low voice Iktomi began to sing. The ducks closed their eyes, folded their wings tightly against their bodies and began to dance. Iktomi sang louder and faster, began moving about the ring. No duck opened its eyes until finally Skiska could stand it no longer and stole the tiniest peek.

He squawked in awful terror. "Run for your lives! Fly away! Iktomi is twisting your heads and breaking your necks!"

The remaining ducks learned a very valuable lesson that day. Never trust someone who does not deserve your trust, even if he promises you something wonderful.

SHE WHO WATCHES

As the Columbia River approached the gorge through the Cascade mountain range it squeezed between basalt cliffs in a torrent of churning white water. At the head of this long chute stood the Klickitat Indian village of Quenett.

The Lewis and Clark journals made note: "Here is the great fishing-place of the Columbia. In the spring of the year, when the water is high, the salmon ascend the river in incredible numbers. As they pass through this narrow strait, the Indians, standing on the rocks, or on the ends of wooden stages projecting from the banks, scoop them up with small nets distended on hoops and attached to long handles, and cast them on the shore."

During the salmon run great numbers of Indians, perhaps 3,000, would gather near Quenett to fish, trade and gamble. From the west came coastal tribes who brought oysters, clams and fish. From the east came Rocky Mountain tribes who brought highly-prized commodities from the plains: horses, buffalo hides and cured meat. It was at Quenett that the Indians of the interior learned that white men in sailing ships had come to the coast. The trinkets and metal pots and knives brought by these traders were in high demand.

Fur traders began using the Columbia River as a highway. They called the long narrow gorge, which they were forced to portage, "La Grande Dalle de la Columbia".

In time the white man built a dam that blocked the river and flooded the Indian fishing grounds and the village of Quenett. All that remained were the Indian pictures on the high basalt cliffs. The largest of these, six feet in diameter, is the face of She Who Watches, *Tsagaglalal*. Her wide eyes stare from a smooth pillar. Where once they watched over the ancient fishing village and the long narrows, they now witness trains rumbling past, river barges plying the flat waters of a man-made lake and I-84 and its steady stream of freeway traffic. No one knows how many thousands of years she has watched.

LUCKY TO BE ALIVE

"You might think this is a tall tale," spoke the old man, "but I know better. Happened long ago. I was living on a place way back in the hills.

"One day I went hunting, knocked down a bull elk. He dropped like a rock but up he jumps and runs away. There was no trouble following the tracks and the trail of blood dropped here and there on rocks and fern leaves. But the bull seemed unfazed as it plowed through thickets and up hillsides, leading me farther and farther from the cabin. I was determined to get that elk and every once in a while I would catch a glimpse of him and manage to snap off a shot.

"It was nearly dark when I finally ran down the bull and used my last shot to kill it. I knew I would be spending the night out there. I gathered wood for a fire and cooked a choice piece of tasty back strap on a willow spit. I was just finishing the last bite when I looked up and directly across the fire from me was a huge, horrible creature with long hair like a bear but the face of a bearded man. The strangest of all was the one eye, big as a saucer, right in the middle of his forehead. It watched my every move, intent, unblinking.

"As the fire began to die the creature leaned forward, toward me. I quickly grabbed a fistful of limb wood, tossed it on the fire. He shrunk back and sat on his haunches.

"There are no words that could adequately describe the terrible feeling that overcame me as I stared into that hideous and hateful eye. All through the black night it watched, waiting for the fire to die or for me to fall asleep. I kept the flames going and prayed out loud that my supply of wood held until morning.

"And then, when I was down to my last sliver of wood, I finally saw the eye shift and look toward the sky. To my great joy the stars were fading, dawn was coming and the terrifying night would finally end.

"When I looked again the monster was gone. It had vanished into thin air. And me, well, I felt lucky to be alive."

JUST A STORY

This story happened many years ago but, according to the fellow who told it, "It just shows you how ghost stories get started.

"Seems this one boy lived back in the woods and every evening he had to go out and bring in the cows. It would be nearly dusk and each time he passed this big tree beside the trail there would be something hanging upside down from a limb.

"This boy told a few of his friends about it. But they didn't believe him. So he bet them, said he would pay off if they went up there and didn't see the thing hanging in the tree.

"Late the next afternoon the boy went up to the tree a little early and watched. But there was nothing to see in the tree. He waited until he heard his friends coming and, not wanting to lose his money, he decided to climb the tree and hang by his knees.

"'Look!' cried one of his friends.

"Another offered, 'I thought he said there was only one. I see two of them.'

"With that the boy in the tree swung his head left and right to see what was hanging next to him and then he dropped to the ground. And, of course, his friends ran off.

"'Wait for me! I'm one of you!' he hollered, chasing after them.

"Two of the boys were running together and one wanted to know, 'What did it say?'

"The other replied breathlessly, 'He said, wait fer me, I'm gonna get one of you.' And the boys ran all the faster."

6

THE DANCE

Spring of 1852 the Missouri River was lined with encampments of wagon pioneers. Those on the west bank were waiting for those on the east side to be ferried across so they could begin the 2,000-mile journey over the Oregon Trail.

A large number of plains Indians had gathered on the west side and during the day they visited the pioneer camps to barter buffalo meat and buffalo robes for food, trinkets and weapons.

One night the Indians built an especially large fire and held a ceremony that involved dancing, chanting, singing and the beating of drums. The pioneers on the east side took notice. They watched the black silhouettes passing back and forth in front of the firelight and came to a hasty conclusion that the Indians were involved in a war dance, and that they would soon attack the white pioneers.

"What can we do to stop it?" someone asked.

"Lob a few bullets in their direction and let those savages know we mean business," he was told.

A witness to the events, A. R. Hawk, wrote: "In order to deter the Indians the excited mob on our side commenced shooting across the river. I don't suppose there was as much powder burned in as short a time at the battle of Bull Run as there was on the banks of the Missouri on that dark night."

During the middle of this barrage a ferryboat, with a company of thirty marksmen, was launched. Mr. Cline was in the company and afterward he told: "It was a difficult and dangerous crossing but the most dangerous part was in attempting a landing while the boys on the east side continued with volley after volley. By the time we set foot on land we were of a mind to wipe out every Indian on the plains.

"Much to our embarrassment we discovered the Indians were not on the warpath. They had just been dancing. And so we left them alone and departed."

The Indians' fire died down. The pile of embers glowed fiercely but that night there was no more dancing.

CURSE OF THE MOTHER LODE

Three young men came west in search of adventure and gold. They found both, and more....

In an isolated valley they located a lone miner, an old man. He warned them, "You'll find gold aplenty, but beware of the curse. I have buried four men.

"If you want to stay alive, make sure you are snug in your tent by nightfall. Don't come out for nothin', not 'til the sun's in the sky."

The young men were skeptical but they decided to play it safe and each night sought refuge in their tent. By day they panned the creek, going farther and farther upstream. In their wanderings they stumbled upon a cabin. Strangely, it was furnished and supplies were neatly stacked on the shelves; but from all indications, it was abandoned. Just below the cabin they found the richest diggings yet and that afternoon one of the boys vowed to spend the night at the cabin instead of returning to camp. The other two tried to talk him out of it but to no avail. He stayed.

The next morning his body was discovered in the doorway of the cabin. His friends buried him and vowed to solve the mystery. They boarded up the windows of the cabin and nailed the doors shut from the inside. As the sun slid from the sky they waited.

They did not have to wait long before they heard a hissing sound. It was coming from an old trunk on the floor. In terror they tore away the nails from the door and escaped into the night.

In daylight they returned and discovered the trunk concealed a shaft. They explored it and found the Mother Lode. Soon after the mystery of the deadly curse was solved.

In addition to the big strike the cabin owner had evidently hit a pocket of deadly cyanide gas. At night, when the barometric pressure changed, the shaft blew deadly gas out the opening.

CASCADE MASSACRE

Upon reaching the Columbia River, Margaret Windsor, an Oregon Trail pioneer of 1852, came down with mountain fever. She was taken to a hospital that had been erected at the head of Cascade Rapids.

When she had recovered Margaret began working at a nearby hotel and it was there she met and married Felix Iman. They took a donation land claim and built a cabin from hewn logs.

As settlers flooded into the country some of the Columbia River Indians became hostile and finally, the morning of March 26, 1856, they went on the warpath. They attacked the sawmill on the upper end of Cascade Portage, killing and scalping a workman, his wife and her younger brother.

Margaret recalled the massacre: "At that time I was sick in bed with a small baby. We were carried from my bed to the river and put into a skiff. It was then I discovered nobody had thought to get my little two-year-old boy, left behind asleep in his bed. He was retrieved by a young man known for his speed as a runner.

"I think that day was the worst I ever witnessed on the old Columbia and there were many, taking it all in all. I do remember that boat ride to safety: the roar of the small cannon at the block house, the firing of guns, the cries of the warriors and the sight of them in their war paint, the screams and moans of the wounded, the smoke of the burning buildings, the splashing waters and the bounding skiff. We landed safely on the Oregon shore and took the steamer *Mary* to The Dalles.

"Later, when we returned to Cascade Portage I hardly knew the place. Buildings, including our cabin, had been burned to the ground.

"Fourteen Indians were captured. They were to be hung from a limb of a tree. Some, when asked to speak of their involvement in the massacre, refused, shook their heads and put the noose about their own necks."

10

GHOST STORY

The campfire settled, sending a cloud of sparks into the dark sky. All of a sudden the hound dog jumped to his feet, hair along his neck stood on end. He growled, but just as suddenly put his tail between his legs and cowered off into the brush.

"What's wrong with him?" the kid wanted to know.

His grandfather told him, "An animal can sense things that a human cannot." He paused for a moment, and then concluded, "Well, I guess you're old enough to hear a ghost story."

Before he said anymore the old man went about rebuilding the fire. Hot orange flames licked the night. He settled himself and began: "When I first came into the country I was riding a gentle mare. She was steady as the Rock of Gibraltar.

"Came through where we are camped now. It was long after dark. Without the least bit of warning, the mare stops dead in her tracks, tenses up and lets out a snort. Then she leaps into a full gallop. All I could do was try and hang on. I was leaned way over, hugging her neck, branches slapping me across the face as she raced lickety-split down the trail.

"At one point I saw a form racing along beside us. It scared me and I hollered out, 'Who's there?' Of course, there was no answer. But I had this cold chill run the length of my spine....

"I finally got the mare stopped and that was it. I never knew if I had seen a ghost or not. Later I mentioned what had happened to a fellow who lived down the road and he told me about an old miner up here who got killed by his partner and every so often, according to the story, his spirit returns to the scene of the crime.... It's just a story. Hope I didn't scare ya'."

"Naw," said the boy. "Didn't scare me one little bit."

Just then the hound dog returned to the campfire and when his cold muzzle touched the boy's hand the boy must have thought he was shaking hands with a dead man. He let out a howl that would curl the hair on a grizzly bear.

11

THIRTEENTH DAY OF JULY

Twin brothers, Sam and Harry Lockhart, were early settlers in the ranching country near Mount Shasta. Local Indians resented the intrusion of the white men and they attacked the small settlement of Shasta and killed every person.

Sam Lockhart was away at the time of the massacre and when he returned and discovered his brother had been killed, he swore undying vengeance against the members of the Pit River tribe he felt were responsible.

Sam took to the hills and one-by-one he hunted down the Indians. Acting as judge, jury and executioner he attempted to avenge his brother's life. Several times federal authorities warned Sam about his indiscriminate killing of Indians and several times he was arrested. But each time, as soon as he was released, he would return to the Mount Shasta area. It was estimated that he killed 25 Indians before he felt he had evened the score and moved on to Silver City, Idaho where he began mining gold.

On the evening of April 1, 1868 Sam was sitting on a bench in front of the stage office. Marion Moore, accompanied by three others, walked up and began arguing with Sam. The two men had been involved in a long-running dispute about a mining claim boundary. Threats were shouted and gunshots were exchanged. Moore was struck by a bullet in the chest. He staggered about fifty steps and dropped dead. Sam was wounded in the left arm. He told his friends that it was nothing but a scratch and invited them to accompany him to the saloon for a drink of whiskey.

A few days later the doctor was called to Sam's room. By then gangrene had set in and the arm had to be amputated. The operation was followed by blood poisoning.

During his final days Sam suffered terribly. He ranted and raved about the Indians and white men he had killed. Finally, on the 13th day of July, the turbulent life of Sam Lockhart came to an end.

MOUNTAIN GRAVE

A few days before Christmas 1877 mail carrier John Templeton Craig departed from Eugene with a blizzard nipping at his heels. He told friends, "I'm going to make a run at it." He was hoping to cross the Cascade Mountains to Camp Polk before the full fury of the storm made travel impossible.

Fifteen years before, while driving cattle to the Willamette Valley, Craig had located a high pass over the mountains. After that he worked to develop the trail into a toll road, living in the mountains, often sleeping in the hollow trunks of trees. With an axe and crosscut saw he hacked out a right-of-way, and laid logs accordion-fashion in the low, boggy spots.

At the 5,300-foot summit of McKenzie Pass, where the road skirted around the edge of a lava flow, Craig built himself a rock cabin. The chimney extended 15 feet in the air, above the highest snow line. Often during winter months Craig would be forced to wait out storms in his summit cabin.

So it was with the Christmas blizzard of 1877. The storm overtook him. The temperature plummeted, wind howled through the big fir trees and snow built layer upon layer. Craig strapped on his snow shoes and climbed up the long ridge that would take him to the summit.

At last he topped out and, finding the chimney sticking above the snow, he dug down to the entrance and pushed open the door. By then he was exhausted and numb with cold.

He kept dry matches and kindling on the hearth and managed to light a fire. As the heat began to warm him he lay down on the hearth and fell asleep. While he slept the snow on his clothing melted, wet the matches and drowned the small fire. Craig awoke, attempted to start another fire, could not, so wrapped himself in a quilt and lay back down.

That spring friends and relatives found the frozen body of John Templeton Craig. They buried him with the cauldron of Black Crater forever his headstone and the knife-edge peak of North Sister marking his feet.

13

MINING CAMP MEMORIES

"I was 11 years old when my family started west in a covered wagon," related Catherine Norville. "We buried my brother Dave, he was but a toddler, along the way.

"We came as far as the Blue Mountains of Oregon. Gold had been struck there the year before, in 1861, and Father took a job as carpenter in the lively mining camp of Auburn.

"How lively was it? I remember one time a gambler by the name of Spanish Tom was arrested for killing two men in a quarrel over a game of cards. He got on his horse and escaped, but was run down and arrested.

"When Spanish Tom was brought in, the miners demanded he stand trial. The event was held out in the open so all who were interested could attend.

"Cap Johnson hopped onto a stump and yelled for justice. He incited the other miners to lynch Spanish Tom. A fellow by the name of Kirkpatrick stood on another stump calling for order and urging that a fair trial be given and Spanish Tom be hung in a lawful manner.

"I remember Spanish Tom standing there before them. He wore a blue flannel shirt, overalls and fine riding boots. A chain was fastened around his ankles. Some from the crowd grabbed the chain and began pulling.

"Sheriff Hall and the men he had deputized tried to hold onto Spanish Tom. The mob pulling on his leg irons won out. They drug him down the street and across Freezeout Gulch, threw a rope over a tree limb and drew him up.

"When the time came for them to cut him down they said they were going to bury him on the hill. I overheard one of the men say, 'What's the use of carrying him clear up there?'

"They dumped Spanish Tom's body down a prospect hole. That was it. I would suppose his bones are still there."

14

AWAY PROSPECTING

The Baker family came to Oregon by covered wagon and took a donation land claim in the Willamette Valley. Rumors soon began circulating that gold had been discovered in California. Mr. Baker made up his mind to leave his family in Oregon and travel to the diggings.

J.A. Baker related that his father "made a great deal of money prospecting for gold in California. One day he met a man who said he was going to the Willamette Valley. Father put about $400 worth of gold into a buckskin pouch and said, 'When you get there look up my wife and give her this.' My mother was very astonished to have a total stranger hand her a pouch of gold dust.

"After mining for a while Father decided to open a store. He sold everything, sugar, flour, tobacco, whatever it was, for a dollar a pound. One time he brought in a big barrel of sauerkraut and a group of German miners pooled their gold dust and bought the whole barrel for a dollar a pound.

"Father told about the time he had bought a pair of new boots for himself, paying $20. He met a miner along the road who signaled for him to stop. He told Father, 'I'll give you seventy-five bucks for your boots if they fit me.'

"Father removed his boots, tossed them to the miner and waited. Presently the miner announced, 'They fit just fine,' and he gave Father $75 in gold dust.

"While we waited for Father to return we worked hard and sacrificed without complaining. I dug potatoes on shares. Every other row was mine. At night I would bring home baskets of potatoes and Mother would pour them in a corner of the cabin. But in the morning the potatoes would be gone. This happened several nights in succession. We could not solve the mystery until finally I crawled under the cabin and discovered wood rats were stealing the potatoes and caching them away for winter."

16

THE HOGS

"When I was a girl my father made me promise that if I ever heard a ghost story I would never repeat it," recalled Annie Perry. "The reason was, my younger sister was deathly afraid of the dark. If she got thirsty in the middle of the night she couldn't even open the door to go out on the porch and get a drink of water from the well. Father didn't want her scared any more. So I never even told her what happened to me with the hogs.

"Where I grew up was back country and in that neck of the woods there were pigs that ran wild. They were mean. Daddy warned me to always stay on the road, never venture off, or else the pigs would get me. I remember he said there was one boy who caught a little pig, made it squeal, and the sow came charging out of the brush, caught him and ate him up. I didn't want that to happen to me.

"When I was seven I started school and had to walk, by myself, to and from the schoolhouse. Coming home that first night, it was storming and almost dark. I was mighty worried about the hogs. I looked this way and looked that. Everything was fine until I came out into a little clearing and right there beside the path I saw this black thing, all humped up, and it looked exactly like a big old hog. I took off running. Ran as fast as I could and the hog never caught me.

"The next morning I had to pass through that clearing again and, oh, I was dreading it. But when I got there, in the daylight, I could clearly see that my hog was actually a burned out stump. But to me, the night before, it had been a hog sure as could be.

"Imagination. And that's exactly how ghost tales get started. If the truth were known there ain't no such thing as ghosts. All the scary things turn out to be stumps or something like that."

THE OLD FREIGHTER

Jesus Urquide was born in Mexico. After gold was discovered in California he traveled north, hoping to strike it rich. He soon discovered more money was to be made in supplying the miners than in mining and he bought a pack string of mules.

Jesus recalled, "I stayed in the Sierra Nevada until gold was discovered in eastern Oregon. I drifted there and ran a 65-mule pack train. After that I went to the mines in Idaho.

"It was up in the Salmon River country that my mules accomplished something no string has ever been able to duplicate. We packed a coil of copper tramway wire weighing 10,000 pounds from Challis to the Yellow Jacket Mine. It was necessary to get this wire to the mine without any breaks, for a splice would have been too dangerous.

"I loaded the wire, spreading out the weight as best I could. Several times a mule would tumble over the side of the mountain, taking coils of wire and other mules with it. Then it was necessary to get them up, repack and start over again. After we made it to the mine, some 70 miles, I swore I would never take another job like that.

"I have packed in the heat and packed in the snow. The closest I came to dying was one time on the Salmon River, during a blizzard. It got dark on me and, with no shelter in sight for my 45 mules, all I could do was to take off the boxes and gather the mules in a circle around me. I managed to make a tiny fire and cook some coffee. The hot drink sustained me.

"In 1912 I had to give up freighting, on account of my eyesight. It was beginning to fail.

"I'm 91 years old now and except for my eyes I'm fit as a fiddle. Guess the 62 years I spent freighting, sleeping five or six nights out of each year in a regular bed, never did any real harm to my health. But stuck in town like I am, not able to get around no more, makes me feel completely lost."

OMAH

There is a legend in the Chetco river country of southwestern Oregon that a mining camp was destroyed by a pack of wild beasts.

According to the story a small settlement was located on a bar where the river made a sharp turn. The place was surrounded by high basalt cliffs. The only one way into camp was down a narrow trail overgrown by towering, mossy oak trees.

Along this trail one of the miners spotted a strange beast. It was ape-like with brown fur and a sloping forehead but it had a human face and a body that was at least eight feet tall. The miner had heard Indians speak of this creature. They called it "Omah".

The beast made a high-pitched whistling sound. There was an answer and it began walking. It had a more graceful walk than a human, bending the knee as it put its weight on it and flowing over the uneven ground. Each stride took it ten or maybe twelve feet.

The miner squeezed off a shot. The creature screamed and tore at its chest. It fell over and death spasms made the arms and legs twitch. And then it was still.

All the forest was quiet. There was not a breath of wind in the trees. The birds did not sing. The frogs, the crickets, the insects, all fell silent.

That evening at camp the miner told his story. He promised in the morning he would take the others and show them the Omah he had killed.

But that night a pack of enraged Omahs attacked the camp. They killed all the miners and knocked down their buildings.

Today all that remains of the camp along the Chetco River are stone foundations hidden in the underbrush and shovels, picks, gold pans and placer mining equipment lying here and there, overgrown by ferns and alder and leopard lilies, azaleas and white bog laurels.

TIMBER WOLVES

"My father and mother crossed the plains to the Willamette Valley in 1853. I was born the winter of 1855," related Jeanette Love.

"The story I wish to relate occurred when I was two years old. We lived in a cabin up Fall Creek. There were plenty of wild animals, bears, wild cats and timber wolves, to contend with.

"The folks had a little flock of sheep. And because of the wild animals, every evening Mother would round up her sheep and bring them to a holding pen beside the cabin.

"This one evening I was left in the cabin while Mother went to bring in the sheep. Grandmother was there with me but I suppose she turned her back and I slipped outside.

"That day the sheep had grazed way down the creek. Mother hiked onto a little wooded knoll where she had a good view, saw that the flock had traveled maybe a half-mile, or so. She would have to work her way down, circle behind and drive them back toward the cabin.

"She took a couple steps, looked ahead and stopped dead in her tracks for only a few feet away were six timber wolves staring hard, lips curled back over their teeth, crouched down low the way wild animals will do when they are ready to attack. Mother was scared. Scared out of her wits but she knew better than to make any sudden motion.

"Slowly, very slowly, she took a step backwards. The timber wolves inched forward and then froze. Mother took several deliberate steps in retreat.

"When Mother was a hundred paces away from the wolves she turned and ran. She fell over me. I had been following her. She grabbed me up and ran, the timber wolves chasing at our heels.

"Mother said she never ran so fast in her life. But she made it. If she had not I most likely would not be alive to tell this story."

INDIAN FIRE

I will tell you how the Indian came to have fire. It happened long ago when the earth was still being made and fire was only to be found at the top of a mountain where the Skookum, the ghost people, guarded it.

They would not share the power of fire. The Indians lived in the lowlands and they were very cold. They would die if they did not have fire. Coyote saw this and he went to the Indians and said, "I will steal fire from the Skookum and give it to you. They will chase me. All the creatures of the woods must help me."

Coyote climbed the mountain, crept quietly forward and hid in a pile of brush where he could watch the fire and the Skookum who guarded it. He waited until the guards were changing places and when their backs were turned to him he dashed in, picked up fire and went racing down the mountain.

The Skookum chased him, caught hold of the tip of his tail. To this day the tip of the coyote's tail is colored white from the touch of the Skookum. Coyote tossed fire to Squirrel.

Squirrel jumped from branch to branch, tree to tree. The fire was very hot and it made Squirrel's tail curve over his back. But still he managed to pass fire to Frog.

Frog took the fire in his mouth and hopped away. Skookum was much faster than Frog and grabbed him by the tail. Frog gave a mighty leap and broke off his tail. That is why frogs have no tail.

Again the Skookum raced after Frog and almost grabbed him when Frog spit out the fire onto Wood. Wood swallowed fire. The Skookum grabbed up Wood and tried in every way to make Wood give up fire. They ranted and raved long into the night but Wood refused to give up fire. Finally the Skookum returned to their cold mountain.

Coyote called all the Indians together. He told them, "I know how to get fire out of Wood." He took two pieces of dry wood and rubbed them together. Fire leaped out of Wood.

A QUESTION OF SANITY

A fellow named Gotschalk arrived in the eastern Oregon town of Pendleton the summer of 1882. From all appearances he seemed perfectly normal and a model citizen. He purchased a home and took an active interest in his community.

But little by little he changed. People began to notice that during a conversation he would suddenly blurt something entirely off the subject and then pick up as though there had been no interruption. That progressed to his muttering words and phrases that were totally inappropriate. He would talk to himself and sometimes, without any provocation, would burst out in hysterical laughter or in crying jags.

Neighbors watched him warily. When he put a For Rent sign in the windows of his home they were relieved. He rented the house and moved his few belongings to a wooden box near the edge of town. He lived there but often could be seen walking around town or standing in the street staring longingly at his former residence.

His strange actions were the subject of much talk and ridicule from the citizens of Pendleton. There were some who said he was harmless and was just going through a spell while others thought he should be taken to the state insane asylum and put away.

Gotschalk made the final decision himself. One day he loaded everything he owned in a wheelbarrow. He pushed it through town and up the hill leading toward the Blue Mountains.

He set camp that night on a flat spot and before he went to sleep he drove a stake in the ground and tied his leg to it with a length of rope, similar to a tethered horse. The following morning he explained his actions to a passerby, saying he walked in his sleep and was afraid he might wander away and not be able to find his way back. Then he loaded his belongs in his wheelbarrow and pushed it toward an unknown destination.

HISTORY BOOK

"The history we read about in books, and history as it really happened isn't at all alike," related Mollie Jett, a pioneer settler on the High Desert.

"Take the Bannock Indian War. I know something about that because my husband and I lived among the Bannocks. White people made promises to the Indians and broke them. If a calf or a horse was stolen it was usually some renegade white man but the blame was always put on an Indian.

"The true story of what happened to cause the war started in 1877. The government had crowded the Bannocks off their land and made them live on the Fort Hall reservation. Under the treaty no one but Indians could set foot on Camas Prairie. That was where the camas root grew which the Indians depended on for food.

"But white men came, turned hogs loose and they rooted up and destroyed the camas. The Indians tried to make the trespassers leave. They refused. So the Indians fired at them and that was the start of the war.

"Egan was chief. He had visited our home frequently. My husband one time even traded him a Henry rifle. That was how much we trusted him. I will say this, he was one of the wisest and most honest men I ever knew.

"Chief Egan told the young men that it was folly to oppose the white man, that in every war with the white man the Indian had lost. But his warriors felt it better to die in battle than to slowly starve to death.

"The Umatilla Indians sent word they would join the Bannocks but they acted with treachery in their hearts. To show their loyalty to the white race, the Umatillas rose up and killed Chief Egan. They took his head and the scalps of nine of his warriors and brought them to Pendleton.

"I felt very sad over Egan's death. And when I read the history books about what they say happened, it makes me all the sadder."

CATCHING BULLETS

Charles Andress was an entertainer who put on a two-bit magic show in drinking establishments throughout the West. At the Bird Cage Theatre in Tombstone, Arizona one of his tricks nearly got him killed.

The Bird Cage Theatre was a famous bar, featuring free-flowing whiskey, painted ladies and a clientele of hard-drinking cowboys, miners, gamblers and gunmen. There was a sign at the door requesting patrons to check their hardware at the bar, but few did. The walls, ceiling and even the huge semi-nude painting of a belly dancer were peppered with bullet holes.

The night Charles Andress stepped on stage the Bird Cage was hot, noisy and smoky. He called out, "Ladies and Gentlemen, may I please have your attention," but the revelers ignored him as he began his act, a performance which included pulling a white rabbit out of a hat and card tricks.

Finally he announced, "Ladies and Gentlemen, tonight you will be treated to one of the world's most amazing feats. I will catch a bullet in my teeth."

He called for his assistant, who came on stage with a six-shooter and walked to within a couple paces of the famous magician. Slowly he raised the pistol with the blank cartridge in the chamber and pointed it directly into the face of Charles Andress. He pulled the trigger, white smoke belched out of the end of the barrel. An ominous clap of thunder echoed off the walls and then a strange quietness fell over the room. All eyes were turned toward the stage watching the star performer stumble backwards, then gain his balance and come forward to spit a lead slug out of his mouth and onto the floor.

This uneasy calm was broken when one of the customers drew his revolver and yelled, "If you're so good, catch this one!" But the bullet missed its mark and crashed harmlessly into the wall. Charles Andress made a quick exit.

SLAVE GIRL

Hugh Eldridge was born on Puget Sound back in the days when the land still belonged to the natives.

Remembering back to that time, he told this story: "My mother came to the north coast in a sailing ship. She was the first white woman in the settlement and upon her arrival she lived in a tiny log cabin and cooked for the crew of Roeder and Peabody, the second sawmill built on the Sound. After she and Father married they moved to a donation land claim.

"One time Father was working and Mother was at home with her two small children. There came a pounding on the door. Mother opened it to a brown-skinned girl who was greatly excited.

"'Calm down,' Mother told her. 'What is it? What is the matter?'

"The girl was near hysterics. She let it be known that she was being pursued. She implored Mother to allow her to come in. She felt she would be safe in the cabin.

"'I can't do that,' Mother told her. 'I just can't do that. My two babies and I are here alone. Don't ask me to hide you. Please don't.'

"Over the girl's begging and pleading Mother could hear the sounds of a large number of Indians coming up the trail and she relented and allowed the girl to come inside the cabin where she promptly secreted herself under the bed.

"The cabin was surrounded by Indians who demanded either the girl or admittance. They were refused but they were able to force an entrance at the back door. The room was quickly filled to overflowing with angry Indians. And it did not take them long to discover the poor girl hiding under the bed.

"They seized her by the hair and dragged her outside and down to their canoes. We later learned that the Indians owned the girl and were just making sure their property did not run away. Her name was Kanaka. She was a Hawaiian and as a child had been brought to the Pacific coast by one of the trading ships and sold into slavery."

26

SEVENTY-FOOT RIATA

Tebo Ortego buckarooed for Pete French on the famous P Ranch. He was known far and wide as the teller of tall tales. But according to Tebo there was one time he had the tables turned, and he got fed the tall tale.

"Happened one summer," he claimed. "There was this wild mustang, palamino stud, a beautiful specimen of a horse, and of course all the High Desert cowboys wanted to catch him. I made up my mind I was going to be the lucky one.

"I figured there was no horse alive that could match the stallion for speed and if I was going to get a noose around its neck I had to first off surprise it and second, have a long rope. So I sat down and braided myself a 70-foot, rawhide riata.

"When it was finished I went looking for the stallion and his band of mares. I spotted them a long way off, just about where I figured they would be, scouted around and discovered they were using a water hole in the back of a box canyon.

"I allowed them to enter it and then stationed myself behind a boulder at the mouth. I waited and waited. Finally I heard the unmistakable sound of horses moving toward me. I shook out a loop and readied myself.

"The stallion stepped out in the open. I made a good throw. The loop settled cleanly over his head. I tried to take my turn around the saddle horn, and even though I had seventy feet to play with, I was just not fast enough. That pretty well demonstrates the speed of that wild stallion.

"I went after him, went just as fast as my saddle horse would carry me. I came to a sheep camp, roused the herder, asked him, 'Seen a palamino stud horse runnin' like the wind?'

"'Sure 'nough did,' claimed the herder. 'Never seen anythin' move so fast. Funny thing was, he had a long riata 'round his neck standin' straight out like it'd been starched.

"'But that wasn't the funniest thing. Funniest thing was that rawhide rope was covered thick with horse flies, just tryin' ta keep up.'"

SKUNK MEAT

Dr. Elijah White came to the Oregon country in 1837. He was a religious man and deeply committed to Christianizing the Indians. But like the other missionaries he found little success.

He returned east in 1840 and it was his good fortune, at a time when national interest was focused on the West, to have the latest information. He gave lectures, describing the country to audiences and calling for families to emigrate to Oregon.

The spring of 1842 Dr. White arrived at the edge of the western frontier and found a group of prospective settlers waiting for someone to lead them west. The ox-train, under his leadership, departed Elm Grove, Missouri on May 16, 1842. Along the way, one by one, the wagons were discarded. The emigrants, on foot and horseback, continued westward and late that fall reached the Willamette Valley.

Dr. White continued to urge immigration to Oregon. In 1845, after wagons had successfully been brought to the Willamette Valley, Dr. White returned to the east. Orris Brown accompanied him on the trip. He told how the Pawnee Indians attacked the small party and robbed them of nearly all their food and possessions. He related: "We went without food until one of the party was successful in killing a skunk. It was cooked over an open fire. Before we could eat Dr. White made quite a display of saying a blessing.

"'I won't stand for such a thing,' I told him. 'Having any blessing over a skunk is too much a sacrilege. If the Lord is as good as you profess Him to be He would furnish us with better meat. We will eat and neither thank Him nor complain to Him.

"'As for you, Dr. White, you better save your blessings until we get deer meat or something fit to eat.' And that was all that was said. We ate our skunk meat in silence."

THE GRAVE

When she was 80 years old Marianne D'Arcy, an Oregon Trail pioneer of 1846, told about the hardships of her life.

"My mother bore 12 children," related Marianne. "She worked hard all her life and died a comparatively young woman. In those early days it was generally the second or third wife who enjoyed the benefits and comforts that had gone into the hard work of establishing the farm and home in the wilderness.

"Death was something we had to take in stride. We knew very little of contagious diseases. One of the very worst years for sickness was 1852. Wagon emigrants brought many diseases with them from across the plains. One of my aunts, Father's sister, came to Oregon that year and her family, upon reaching the Willamette Valley, was still suffering from mountain fever, the name given to what we now call typhoid.

"Since the family had nowhere to go they moved into our home. All was fine for a while, a week or more, and then, one by one, us children came down with the disease. The doctor was sent for but there was very little he could do. He said the fever had to run its course.

"My brother Horton and sister Josephine and I were very, very ill. In fact, the doctor said there was no saving us and he directed Father to prepare our graves. He did this, digging three holes side-by-side in the soft earth.

"Horton was the first to go. He was laid to rest. Next was Josephine. The grave between was intended for me. But I surprised them all. I did not die. Slowly and steadily my condition improved.

"It was not until a quarter of a century later that the spot between Horton and Josephine was finally put to use. I buried my own son in the grave that had been dug for me."

PREMATURELY GRAY

"Along in the 1870s, while courting a special girl, a rather amusing incident befell me," recalled Kelsey Congor.

"At the time I was riding a rather flighty mare. She was a good horse, but at some point during the day, out of the clear blue and I never knew when, she would commence bucking.

"This one day in particular I was crossing through the back country on the way to visit my girl. "Along the way the trail crossed a slough divided by a narrow island. As we came up on the island, and the mare had solid ground under her feet, she humped her back and began bucking. There was absolutely nothing I could do and I was unceremoniously bucked off.

"I lost my hat and I will admit to losing my temper, too. I had a few choice words for the mare and then recovered my hat and remounted. I rode directly to my girl's house, knocked on the door and her mother answered.

"'What happened to you?' she wanted to know.

"'I got bucked off,' I said.

"'Come on in. Stand over by the fire,' she told me.

"It was several minutes before my girl entered the room. By then my clothes were steaming from the heat of the fire. She came directly to me and with a smile tugging at the corners of her mouth she greeted me with, 'Kelsey, you are much too old for me. You are getting gray.'

"Immediately I ran my fingers through my hair and to my utter embarrassment found it plastered with sand. I explained my hat had been full of sand and water when I found it and though I shook it out, enough sand had stayed that it made my hair appear gray.

"My girl simply laughed at my discomfort. Later she and I married and she never allowed me to forget the time I was prematurely gray."

BURIED ALIVE

In 1852 the 4th Infantry received orders to travel from the east coast to Fort Vancouver in the Oregon Territory. The soldiers and their families boarded a ship and set sail for Panama.

The ship reached the Isthmus but there were delays in crossing to the Pacific side. During the wait many of the soldiers and the women and children became sick with cholera. More than one-third would die.

Oftentimes the single men who died would have no mourners to attend their funeral. But Fanny Kelly, a sensitive and tender-hearted fourteen-year-old daughter of a soldier, thought every person deserved a proper ceremony. To Fanny that meant the attendance of at least one mourner. She became the official mourner at the funerals of those who had no family.

One time the canvas sack containing the body of a soldier was about to be lowered into the ground when Fanny thought she saw the canvas move. She hollered, "Stop! I think that man is alive."

"He can't be," said a soldier. "The doctor pronounced him dead."

"I saw him move. Open it up. Please. Please, open it," pleaded Fanny.

The soldier finally relented. He withdrew his knife and cut the stitches to the canvas bag. Fresh air rushed inside and revived the man who moaned and began trying to move his arms. The canvas was quickly cut away and the man, a Scotsman named Thompson, was set free.

Years later Fanny was visiting Fort Vancouver. One of the soldiers rushed to her. It was Thompson. "You are the little girl to whom I owe my life," he told her. "If it had not been for you I would be lying in a grave on the Isthmus, like so many others. You kept me from being buried alive."

POTATO PATCH GOLD

"I'm dying. I want to confess and wipe the slate clean," the old man whispered from his death bed.

"It was in 18 and 72. My partner and I robbed the Jacksonville stage, stole the gold shipment, escaped into the Cascade Mountains.

"We were afraid the posse would catch us, so we traveled day and night. Crossed over to the Klamath Basin, skirted around the settlement of Linkville. A day's ride east of there we stopped at a stage station, ate what the family living there could spare and spent the night. In the morning we went a short distance from the cabin and buried the gold.

"Not long after that my partner got in a fight and was killed. I kept running, never went back.

"Get me a paper and pen. I'll draw a map."

The old man made scribble marks on the paper to show the location of the mountains, Linkville and the stage station. He drew an oval and made the notation, "Potato Patch".

He rested for a moment and then told, "There was a fenced-in area, a tall fence, eight feet high, to keep out the deer. They were growing potatoes there.

"My partner and I got up early, took the gold, hiked down along the fence and stepped off two hundred and twenty paces, to a spot where four trees were growing close together like fingers on a hand. From the tree closest to the cabin we measured off nine paces and took two more paces at a right angle. Here we dug a hole and buried the gold. We rolled a big rock on top of it so as to hide the fresh-turned earth."

He made an X on the map, said, "Right here is where you will find it. Now my conscience is clear." That night the old man died in his sleep.

The details of his original map have been reproduced countless times, and though treasure seekers have tried to locate the hiding place, no one has yet discovered the spot where nearly fifty pounds of gold were buried so many years ago.

GOING HOME

The winter of 1879 dragged on and on. Finally Wallowa Valley rancher H.K. Chamberlain had to make a run to the Grande Ronde Valley for supplies.

He was returning home with his sleigh when a chinook wind hit, melting the snow. The resulting runoff pushed the rivers to flood stage. Chamberlain was left stranded at the meeting of the Wallowa and Minam rivers; the bridge had washed out.

Jack Graham operated the stage station at Minam and Chamberlain stayed with him to wait for the water to recede. Sure enough, the warm wind died and the air became cold and still. During the night it snowed a fresh blanket and the river began to recede.

The following morning Graham told his guest, "Come with me and see my pigs." As they neared the barn there was a surprised squeal. A second later the men spotted a cougar bounding through the snow with one of the small pigs in his jaws. The men ran back to the house for their rifles and with Graham's hunting dog they took up the trail of the cougar.

The cougar had crossed the river and Graham urged his dog to follow. At first it was reluctant to brave the icy water but after encouragement it plunged in and swam to the other side. After a few moments the hound began baying that the cat was treed.

"Has he ever been wrong?" Chamberlain wanted to know.

"Never," stated Graham and the two men waded across the waist-deep water, holding their rifles above their heads. On the other side they found the cougar 20 feet up a pine tree. They shot him, took the pelt and recrossed the river.

DAVY CROCKETT

Settlers at Puget Sound gave the chief of the Lummi Indians the name Davy Crockett. Late one afternoon he visited the settlement with a warning that a band of hostile Indians from British Columbia was planning a surprise attack.

"He's always been straight with us," said one of the white men. "We best prepare ourselves."

Two men were sent out in a canoe to act as sentinels. The sun dropped from the sky and the surface of the bay became calm and as flat as a sheet of glass. It grew very dark and then, finally, the moon emerged and cast a pale glow of yellow light.

In the settlement Davy Crockett was telling stories about the band of Indians from British Columbia, saying they were the most warlike of all the natives. He said that they raided villages along the coast, killing the men and taking women and young girls as slaves.

One of the white men accidently set off his flintlock musket and even before the echo could bounce back there came an avalanche of shrill war whoops and a volley of rifle shots. The other settlers abandoned their cabins, took to their heels and fled to the safety of the deep woods.

But Davy Crockett and his brother, Yellow Kanin climbed up a small bluff that overlooked Bellingham Bay. They could make out two war canoes attempting to land on the beach at the settlement. They fired their rifles, the canoes retreated. That night, time after time, the hostile Indians attempted to land and each time were repulsed by Davy Crockett and Yellow Kanin.

In the morning the white people emerged from the woods. The enemy was gone. The settlement was intact. But evidence of what might have been had washed up on shore; the canoe and the bodies of the two white sentinels.

WILD CATTLE

The Spencer family were pioneers of 1848 who settled in the Willamette Valley. The children, Joe, Laura and little Angelica, attended school in a one-room log structure. Each morning they walked two miles to school and each evening they trudged two miles home.

One afternoon Joe ran ahead while his sisters were still walking along at the edge of the open meadow and the deep, dark forest. Angelica was trying to catch a yellow butterfly that flitted from wildflower to wildflower. Laura tagged along.

It was Laura who first noticed the cattle. In those days the country was open and unfenced. A neighbor had brought in a herd of Spanish, long-horned cattle. They were wild and dangerous and Mr. Spencer had warned, "You kids give those cattle a wide berth."

On that afternoon the cattle were attracted by something, perhaps Angelica's new dress, made by her mother from bright red cloth. Years later Laura recalled the incident, saying, "Father always told us that in case of danger we were to stand our ground and never run. And that was what we did.

"From every direction the cattle began running toward us. I squeezed Angelica's hand, whispered, 'Don't move!'

"The cattle put their noses close to the ground and shook their heads and their long horns at us. They sniffed and snorted, pawed at the ground and kicked up dirt over their backs. All the while my sister and I stood as still as two little church mice. We never so much as blinked an eye.

"Presently the cattle gave up. I suppose we were not much fun for them. After they were gone Angelica and I, slipping from one tree to the next, made our way home.

"We told Father what happened and he shook his head and said, 'You did the right thing. If you had moved they would have run you down, pawed you to death and trampled you into the ground.'

"And I believe they would have."

COMING WEST

"In March of 1863, with the intention of traveling the Oregon Trail, I bought a wagon," related J.B. Wright, a resident of Dorris County, Iowa.

"Upon the advice of pioneers who had been over the trail I made some modifications to my wagon. First, I put an extra decking about 15 inches above the wagon bed where I placed my stores and supplies. On the decking was a mattress for sleeping.

"At the back of the wagon I attached a grub box with a double lid. When opened, this double lid made a table and when the lid was folded up three chairs could be roped to it.

"Crossing the plains, the thing that made the biggest impression on me were the bleached and whitened bones of the buffalo. The summer before there had been a drought and thousands of buffalo perished for want of water. The shoulder blades and broader bones had been autographed and used as calling cards by the emigrants who preceded us.

"We reached South Pass on July 8. The grade was so gradual it was hard to realize we had climbed to the top of the Rocky Mountains. While going down the slope toward Green River we met 400 Indians who were on the war path against their neighbors, the Utes. A wagon train near us was attacked, some of their animals were run off and one man was killed.

"On our way west our narrowest escape from death occurred along the Snake River. We camped in a dry gulch, on a knoll where there was a spring. A rain came up sudden and we took shelter in the wagon. A few moments later I lifted the flap, looked out and saw a column of water five feet high rolling toward us. Fortunately we had camped on the knoll and were above the water's path or we surely would have been swept away."

THE BURIAL

The herring industry on the North Pacific coast had gone bust but a group of old bachelors hung on at the camp in Halibut Cove. They lived off the land, planting gardens, fishing for salmon and hunting ducks, geese and wild game. In the dead of winter one of the men, John Leiren, died suddenly. The door to his cabin was propped open and the body allowed to freeze. John was a big man, weighing over 300 pounds. The cot where he was laid to rest sagged under his weight and when the men tried to place John in a hastily-built coffin, they discovered he would not fit.

"I got an idea. You fellars sit on the lid and I'll try and nail it shut," offered Bud Wilkins.

When that job was completed the men sat around drinking John's stash of home brew and discussing what should be done. After all, they could not dig a hole in the frozen ground. It was Rusty Linn who came up with the solution. Near his cabin he had dug a well, a well into which saltwater had seeped, making it worthless. He suggested, "It's about the right size. Let's stuff him down there."

The men drug the casket to the well. They toasted their departed friend with, "Here's to old John and down the hatch." Eventually they got around to the burying part of the ceremony.

It took all of the men working in unison to lift the head of the casket up and tip the foot into the opening of the well. But because the boards had been bowed around the body, the casket would not fit. The men wiggled it back and forth, it slipped a few inches and then, with a whoosh, slid to the bottom of the well.

In the years since the winter burial the men have all passed away; the camp at Halibut Cove has been abandoned, the cabins rotted to nothing. The alder and devil's club have taken over, covering any trace of where John Leiren stands for eternity.

REMEMBERING CHIEF JOSEPH

"I'll tell you about Chief Joseph. He was a friend of mine, a respected friend," related pioneer Barney Owsley.

"Chief Joseph never made any trouble. He asked only that his tribe, the Nez Perce, might dwell in the Wallowa Valley of Oregon. It had been given to Old Chief Joseph in the treaty of 1855. It was an ideal place for anybody, white or red. There were trout and salmon for the catching and elk and deer to be hunted. There was small game of every description. In the spring there were roots and berries. The valley was sheltered in winter, cool in summer, and nothing more was needed or desired by the Nez Perce.

"White men coveted this paradise. The government ordered the Indians to leave. They refused. Soldiers were sent to enforce the order. They were ambushed and the war was on.

"At the time I was operating a pack train, carrying supplies to the miners in the mountains of Idaho. I brushed into the retreating Nez Perce warriors and managed to escape with my skin, but I had no choice but to desert my pack train.

"I crawled into a thicket. I stayed hid all that day, that night and the sun was well up before I ventured out.

"The Indians were gone. I searched for my horses and, much to my surprise, found my cargo largely intact. Except for a whiskey barrel. It had been tapped and considerable of the contents had been consumed.

"I joined the company that was organized to bring in Joseph and his band. I did scouting duty hoping to have an opportunity to speak to Joseph, but of course that was impossible and I gave up on the Middle Fork of the Clearwater River.

"The Nez Perce continued, keeping up a running fight as they retreated. General Miles finally surrounded Chief Joseph and his small band near the Canadian Border at Bear Paw Mountain. They were forced to surrender.

"I never saw Chief Joseph again."

OLD JACK

"Grandma and Grandpa Thomas came over the Oregon Trail and settled on Spokane Prairie," related Erma Cameron. "They said in those days the prairie was covered with wild strawberries and driving a wagon across it would make the wheels run red from strawberry juice.

"After they were there a few years they got a dog, an Irish wolfhound they named Old Jack. When he was a pup a wolf bit him through the hips and Grandpa was going to put him out of his misery but the kids pleaded, said they would doctor him back to health and they did.

"Ever after Old Jack was very protective of the kids. One time Grandma caught a tramp with long, dirty whiskers drinking out of her butter churn. She yelled at him to get out and threatened to call Grandpa. The tramp laughed at her, said he had seen Grandpa leave early that morning.

"Grandma called Old Jack and he came through the doorway like a shot, knocked the tramp on the ground and held him by the throat until the fellow begged Grandma to call him off and promised he would leave. Old Jack followed the man a long way down the railroad track before he turned around and came home. Another time the kids were in the front yard playing when a tramp tried to get in the gate. Old Jack wouldn't allow him to set foot inside. When he realized he couldn't get by the dog, he gruffly told the kids to get their mother to call off the dog and fix him something to eat because he was hungry.

"Grandma told him, 'If Old Jack doesn't want you inside then neither do I. But I will fix you a sandwich and bring it out to you.' Old Jack would not allow her to hand the sandwich to the tramp. She had to set it on the gatepost and back away.

"When Grandpa got home he told Grandma he had been worried sick about her and the children and went on to relate the reason for his concern. It turned out a tramp coming through the country had killed an entire family just up the road."

THE FISHING TRIP

"My father was a United States marshal," recalled Otto Walker. "He ranged up and down the west coast. When he was not working he and I would go off into the back country, anywhere there was a good fishing stream.

"The summer of 1903, I was thirteen years old at the time, Father and I went on a fishing trip into the Sierra Nevada. We fished the Truckee River near its quiet beginning at the outlet of Lake Tahoe. Father told me, 'I will fish the far side of the stream and you fish this side. We will meet back in camp at dusk.'

"I fished along and the river dropped into a canyon punctuated with long stretches of roaring white water. Late in the afternoon I started back. Arriving at camp I built a fire, prepared supper and waited for Father. It grew dark and I built a big fire so he would be able to locate camp. All night I kept the fire going.

"Early the next morning I crossed the river and followed it for many miles. I figured Father had fallen and broken his leg but I could not find any trace of him. I returned to camp at dusk, built up the fire and kept it going a second night. By morning I was sick with grief but I went out and looked all that day. And that night, again, I kept vigil at the fire, hoping against hope Father would come stumbling in out of the dark.

"The fourth day two fisherman came across me. They took me to town. A search party was organized and at the end of the second week they located my father's body. It was never known whether he fell into the stream and was drowned or whether some of the enemies he had made in carrying out his duty as United States marshal had killed him and thrown him in the raging river.

"For me all that mattered was the sad fact I no longer had a father."

THE BABY

"So you want me to tell ya the story 'bout the graveyard baby," drawls Grandpa to the kids surrounding his rocking chair. Grandpa lights his pipe and the flame casts an eerie light on his face before the night rushes in again. He puffs and he rocks and the board floor squeaks under his weight. Finally he begins to speak. "This here story is absolute true. I was there. Seen it with my own two eyes.

"What happened is we had this neighbor an' him an' his wife lived up the road, right across from the graveyard. An' this one time he wakes up in the middle of the night hearin' a baby cryin'. Gets up, goes outside, listens real good an' can tell right away the sound is comin' from over yonder in the graveyard.

"He tries to go back to sleep but, of course, he can't. He thinks he's goin' crazy. He's pretty spooked. So he wakes up his wife, she was a barren woman, couldn't have no kids, an' asks her if she hears anythin'. The baby cries again.

"'Where's it comin' from?' she demands to know.

"'Graveyard,' he tells her.

"Even after it got light an' the sun come up they could sometimes hear the baby cry. 'Bout mid-mornin' they come down the road to our place and the man, he tells Pa what they heard an' says, 'I'm 'fraid to go look. You?'

"'Naw,' Pa told 'em. 'I ain't afraid. I'll go over there.'

"Pa, he goes to the graveyard and finds a wicker basket there atop a flat tombstone. An' inside he finds a baby. He totes it across the road and tells the man and woman, 'It's a baby boy.'

"The couple raised the baby up like it was their own. Named him Billy Tombs, after the tombstone where he was found. He was quite a bit younger'n me but in later years I played with 'im a time or two. Billy Tombs. Yep, that was his name. Billy Tombs."

43

SKOOKUM LAKE

There is a lake near the Pacific Ocean surrounded by deep, dark woods. One night an Indian who lived on one side of the lake went to visit a girl who lived on the opposite side.

He pushed off from shore in his canoe, dug in the blade of his paddle and when he pulled it out the spot was marked with a tight whirlpool. Water dripped off the raised paddle. Again he dug it into the black water where moonlight sparkled and shimmered and stars reflected pinpoints of light. A loon called, lonely and haunting. An owl whoo-whooed.

Suddenly the water around the canoe erupted and huge, hideous tentacles closed around the canoe and pulled it under. As quickly as they were thrust above the surface the tentacles retreated, and water covered the horror of what had happened. But for long seconds eerie screams echoed back and forth across the lake, each scream lacking some of the intensity of the previous one. And finally all was ominously quiet.

The Indians were very superstitious and to appease the evil spirit of the lake they began beating drums and chanting. The drums became louder. They danced, faster, faster, and as the dancing reached a frenzy of sound and motion, once again the tentacles broke the surface. The evil spirit stole one of the dancers and retreated to the murky depths.

From that night on the Indians called this place Skookum Lake, meaning place where the evil spirit resides, and no longer did they camp there. When the white man came he changed the name to Devil's Lake.

THE KIDS AND THE CAT

"I was born in 1854 in the little settlement of Portland, Oregon. My brothers and I used to walk from our cabin into town to go to school," recalled Mary Marquam.

"Generally I would be the one to carry the lunch pail while my brothers, Gus and Will, would ride stick horses.

"One day, on the way to school, there was a big yellowish-brown animal standing in the trail. Gus took the stick horse he had been riding and told the beast, 'Get out of our way, you big ugly dog.' He gave it a whack across the back.

"It jumped to one side and acted hurt. Feeling sorry for it, I walked up and gave it a pat on the head, apologized to it for my brother's action. It made a purring sound and I said, 'Why this is not a dog. It's a cat.'

"Gus laughed and said, 'No, it's gotta be a dog. There ain't no cat that big.'

"The animal was friendly to me. It very much wanted to smell the lunch and I had to hold it over my head to protect the basket I carried. Even still, it reached up with its nose to smell it. Suddenly it stopped, turned its head down the trail, stiffened and gave a mighty jump onto a snag. It climbed way up, gave a look around in all directions and then leaped to the ground and disappeared into the underbrush.

"Within a few minutes we were met by our neighbor Albert Kelly. Gus told him about the 'big brown dog'. I said, 'It wasn't a dog, Mr. Kelly. It was a cat.'

"Mr. Kelly had us show him the tracks and he exclaimed, 'Those are the largest cougar tracks I have ever seen. Thank God, that cougar ate nearly a quarter of beef hanging in my barn or he surely would have eaten you children.'

"Not long after that a local merchant, Mr. Murhardt, treed this cougar. And it proved to be one of the largest cats ever killed in the area."

THE BLUFF

The spring of 1861 the Gray family gave up the homestead they had taken in the Okanogan country and started south. William Gray, who was 16 years old at the time, recalled, "Father loaded our belongings on a boat, but the river trip was so dangerous it fell to me to take the family overland.

"We reached a point where the Yakima River empties into the Columbia. That night I staked my riding horse, as usual, near camp and turned the others loose to graze. During the night the Snake River Indians drove our horses off. We were stranded with no way of continuing our journey. I did the only thing there was to do, follow the trail of the stolen horses and try to get them back.

"I followed their tracks for 12 miles and came to a big Indian camp with many tepees. I rode up to a lodge where could be heard the sounds of the tom-tom and Indians dancing. I put on a bold front; dismounted, threw back the flap and stepped into the entrance. The Indians stopped dancing and looked intently at me. I talked the Chinook jargon as well as I did English and I said, 'Some of you have stolen my horses. If they are not back in my camp I will see that every horse in your band is shot.' Utter silence.

"I stepped back, dropped the flap, mounted my horse and started for camp. I had not gone far when four Indians, whooping and howling, overtook me and just before they reached me they divided, two going on each side. I never looked at them. The only way I could carry out my bluff was to appear perfectly fearless.

"When I arrived at camp my mother was crying and said she had been praying for me. As I sat down to my delayed meal I was interrupted by the noise of running horses. Our horses, covered with lather, charged into camp and I hurried out, caught them, staked them, came back and finished my meal. Then we saddled up, loaded the pack animals and continued on our way."

MAN EATER

William Meyers was a concrete mixer by trade. The spring of 1910 found him living at home with his folks and working days, pouring concrete to build the Mount Tabor reservoir for the City of Portland, Oregon.

At 10 o'clock, on the morning of April 18th, a drive chain jumped off the sprocket wheel on the concrete mixer. The safe way would have been to shut down the machinery but the job was running behind schedule and, besides, Meyers had fixed the machine many times before without shutting off the engine.

He tried it this time, picking up the chain and looping it over the sprocket. His glove seemed to catch. At first it was a gentle tugging but within an instant pain shot from Meyers's trapped hand, up his arm and through his entire body. He screamed, tried to pull back but the relentless machine paid him no mind as gear by gear it gobbled up his fingers, and then his hand, wrist....

John Mingler, who was working nearby, heard the terrifying screams and ran toward the concrete mixer. He pulled out his pocketknife and went work hacking away at Meyers arm.

Mingler managed to cut Meyers loose and he fell backwards. Meyers took one look at the bloody stub and fainted dead away. First aid was administered and Meyers was loaded on a streetcar.

The streetcar was met on Grand Avenue by a Red Cross ambulance but the ambulance was delayed twelve minutes when the tender raised the Burnside bridge so a ship could pass. At last Meyers arrived at the hospital where doctors trimmed and sewed up the stump.

Meyers had come as close as is possible to being eaten alive, one bite at a time. And out at Mount Tabor the concrete mixer never missed a stroke as the sprocket wheel whirled and the chain drive clanked and clattered.

48

WRONG DEAD MAN

J.C. Overture was a disturbed young man. He had fought in World War I, distinguished himself for his bravery, and had returned home with great joy and optimism, only to discover his girlfriend, Isabel, had run off with another man.

For a time Overture lived on skid road in Seattle but soon he drifted to Portland where he took cheap rooms and drank cheap booze. His existence was a downward spiral until the day he finally took his own life.

Police found the body and with it a suitcase bearing the identification of William Hogan of Union, Oregon. They made a hasty assumption that the suicide victim was Mr. Hogan. The body was put in a casket and shipped directly to Union.

The Oregonian newspaper printed an obituary for William Hogan, identifying the fact that he had killed himself by his own hands. This news came as a great shock because the family and friends of William Hogan had always considered him to be very stable, an exemplary citizen and a pillar of the community.

"I cannot believe it," claimed one man.

Another said, "Well, you know he was on his way to Seattle. He had to pass through Portland. They found his suitcase and his identification with the body. Anything is possible, I suppose."

When the body arrived in Union authorities opened the casket. The first witnessed proclaimed, "Yep, that's Hogan."

But the others pointed out the fact the dead man was much too young to be Mr. Hogan and, besides, the two men looked very different. The body was positively identified as not belonging to Mr. Hogan. It was promptly returned to Portland.

The mystery was solved on the very day William Hogan was scheduled to be buried. On that day he returned to Union. He assured the townfolks he was in the pink and that all the confusion was caused by the fact a bum had stolen his suitcase from the depot as he was passing through Portland.

HATHAWAY JONES

Hathaway Jones was a mule packer by trade but he is best known as a teller of tall tales. One time *The Oregonian* newspaper named someone else "Liar of the Year" and Hathaway sued for libel and defamation of character.

"I think up my little yarns while travelin' the lonely trails of the Rogue River drainage," Hathaway told an interviewer.

"Take for instance the time I was runnin' a pack string of eight mules. We was haulin' flour ta the folks at the settlement of Agness. Got caught in a snow storm. Heck of a snow storm.

"We had ta take shelter in the hollowed out trunk of a fir tree, big fir tree it was. Room fer me, a fire an' all the mules could have their heads inside out of the weather.

"I went to sleep that night an' when I woke the snow was nine feet deep. Well, sir, I knowed for a solid fact if I didn't get out of there me an' those mules was goin' starve ta death - least ways the mules was gonna starve.

"I slung the packs on the mules an' started 'em 'round the tree. I drove 'em, used the whip an' they was goin' faster, an' faster, an' faster. 'Round an' 'round.

"They ran so fast they started in sweatin'. An' so I swung 'em wide. When they hit that snow bank a cloud of steam boiled like a volcano eruptin'. I lined 'em out, headed 'em down hill an' they ran clear ta Agness. The flour never even got damp."

WHITE ROCK

An old fellow named Brooks used to tell a story about a man who was killed just down the road from his house. He related, "On the way to town I had to pass the spot where it happened. The man, he was killed sitting on the seat of a wagon and was pushed out onto a big white boulder. His blood never did wash off. And every time I passed that white rock it always got to my nerves.

"One night, it was dark and raining, I came home and I could have gone around but it would have been way out of my way so I decided to take my chances with the white rock. When I got pretty close to where the rock was my horse snorted, perked his ears up and stood stiff like a board. I gave him rein but he didn't move a muscle. I clucked to him a time or two. Nothing. I knew if I touched him with the spurs he would have to move and he did, jumping stiff-legged to the side of the road. He bowed his back up like an alley cat. Between my knees I could feel him shakin' a little.

"'Bout that time a flash of white came sliding off the bank to where the rock was and stopped. Scared? Yep, I admit I was scared.

"My horse he figured it out before I did. He probably smelled it. He started taking cautious steps toward the thing and I fidgeted in my coat pocket for a match. In them days there wasn't such things as flashlights. I struck the match, held it out in front of me and there beside the white rock sat a big white shepherd dog.

"At the time I was too serious but afterward I laughed about being so scared. If I hadn't discovered the dog I would have always swore I had seen a ghost."

SECRET PASS

For a half-century Jim Beckwourth roamed the interior west as a mountain man, explorer, scout, soldier and even the chief of an Indian tribe. In 1847 he set out to see the Pacific Ocean.

The Sierra Nevada and a howling blizzard blocked his travel. He turned downhill and stumbled into the protected valley carved by the Feather River. It was free of snow and so lush and inviting that he spent two years trapping there.

When he once again started west, he discovered his valley was actually a secret pass through the mountains. He came to Marysville, a bustling mining town, and called the city fathers together. He described to them his wonderful new pass. With their backing he promised to make Marysville the celebrated ending spot for all those emigrants who traveled the Oregon Trail and swung south over the California Cut-Off.

Beckwourth traveled east with the intention of diverting emigrants. Along the way he was stricken with a high fever and became so sick he crawled off into the brush to die. On the third day he heard voices and was rescued by scouts from a wagon train. The pioneer women nursed him back to health and in return he led them to Marysville. Their arrival kicked off a celebration so wild that when a fire started it went unnoticed. It was soon burning out of control and practically the entire town burned to the ground.

The following morning the mayor informed Beckwourth Marysville would be rebuilt. He said the citizens would be forever grateful for the road to their doorstep, but there would be no money available to pay for it.

Beckwourth said of the mayor, "I felt like scalpin' the mealy-mouthed ol' buzzard, but there warn't no point of it. Ain't no way of stoppin' folks from usin' my road. As fer as me, well, I always did want to see the Pacific Ocean. Reckon that's whar I'll go."

STEALING A BABY

"When we crossed the plains in 1845 I was a baby in my mother's arms, barely six months old. According to the story told to me, I came dangerously close to staying on the plains and never making it to Oregon," related Mary Ann Taylor.

"Seems like along a river someplace our wagon train laid over so the women could wash the dirty clothes that had accumulated and the oxen could rest a bit and fill up on the grass growing along the banks.

"An Indian woman visited camp. I was on a blanket on the ground. Most babies tend to be afraid of strangers but I never was. So when the woman held out her hands to me, to pick me up, I happily went to her. She held me and asked Mother, 'How much it cost, buy your baby?'

"'My baby is not for sale,' Mother said emphatically.

"The Indian woman was not to be denied. She saw her chance the moment Mother turned her back; she scooped me up in her arms and ran for the timber, maybe a half mile away.

"'My baby! My baby,' screamed Mother. 'She stole my baby!'

"With all the commotion Mother created the men were quick to act, coming on the run. Mother pointed toward the retreating figure of the Indian woman and told the men, 'Catch her. She has my baby.'

"In the ensuing foot race the men were much faster. They caught the Indian woman just as she reached the timber and wrestled me free. The woman put up a vigorous protest, saying I was her baby, but of course it was plain to see, as fair and white-skinned as I was, that I could not be an Indian baby.

"I was brought back to camp and returned to Mother. From then on, whenever there were Indians around, Mother never turned her back on me."

LAID TO REST

Willy lived an ordinary life, ranching and farming along the border between Oregon and Idaho. It was after his death that the real mystery began to evolve.

Willy died in 1889. True to his last wishes his friends buried him on his home place. They dug the grave on a peaceful knoll overlooking the meandering Malheur River.

Seven years passed and the estate was purchased by M.G. Hope who hired two men to dig up Willy's coffin. He told them, "I don't want to share my place with the dead. Get him out of here, take him in and bury him at the cemetery in Vale. That's where they should have planted him in the first place."

The men, using picks and shovels to break loose the hard ground, dug down to the coffin. It was still in good condition. They cleaned off the lid.

"Why don't we take a peek inside," suggested one of the men.

"Whatever for?" asked the other.

"Just for a look-see. He's dead, ain't he? Not gonna bother him none. 'Sides, you ever seen a man when he's been in the ground seven years? Ain't ya a little bit curious in what you're gonna look like? Come on, help me."

They pried loose the lid, lifted it up and set it aside. There was Willy. He was turned on his side, his left arm tucked under his head like a pillow and there was a good three inches of beard on his face.

"Oh merciful God!" cried one of the men. They replaced the lid, jumped on the buckboard and raced off to find Frank Glenn, who had been one of Willy's closest friends and had assisted in the burial.

Glenn told the two grave diggers, "When we placed the body in the coffin Willy was clean-shaven. We laid him flat on his back, hands folded over his chest. Now tell me, why are you asking and what seems to be the trouble?"

SASQUATCH

One minute John Mackentire was there, hunting in the foothills of the Cascade Mountains with friends, and the next he had vanished off the face of the earth. Search parties were quickly organized but no trace of the man was ever found.

It was four years later that a party of deer hunters was making a drive in the general area where Mackentire had mysteriously disappeared. One of the men, Mr. Fitzgerald, had been friends with Mackentire.

At one point Mr. Fitzgerald saw movement at the head of a small clearing. He thought it resembled a man and then somehow it reminded him of his missing friend. He called out, "John! John, is that you?"

Later Mr. Fitzgerald told the other hunters what happened next. "When I called out, the figure stood upright. It appeared to be wearing some sort of fur clothing. It just stood there looking at me for the longest time, then turned and strolled away, walking on two legs like a man."

"Well, was it John Mackentire?" one of the hunters demanded to know.

Mr. Fitzgerald shrugged. "I don't know. I just don't know. It looked like a man but it looked like a wild animal, too."

Another of the hunters offered, "If it was John and he is alive he must be in a deranged state. Why else would he stay hidden and live off the land for so long. Can you imagine how tough it would be living out here through the winter?"

"Better forget about hunting," Mr. Fitzgerald told the others, "and concentrate our efforts on locating John. It is a pity to think of him wandering around stark-raving mad."

For several days the men combed the area, searching for any clues, but found nothing. In later years some people have speculated that Mr. Fitzgerald, that fall day in 1885, was the first white man in Oregon to see Sasquatch.

WHERE THE GHOST LIVES

A winter storm in 1874 brought a mystery ship to the Oregon coast. She put in at Yaquina Bay. The captain came ashore, claimed his daughter was not a good sailor in rough weather and rented her a room.

His daughter, Zina, was a raven-haired princess and in the days that followed she spent long hours walking the beach. During Christmas vacation a group of college students rented rooms at the Yaquina Bay hotel. They played on the beach and at night built driftwood bonfires, sang songs and told stories. Before long Zina was included in their fun.

It was Zina who suggested the group visit the abandoned lighthouse that stood at the mouth of Yaquina Bay. "They say it is haunted," she told them.

As the boys and girls neared the lighthouse an ocean breeze covered the bright sunshine with a gloomy fog. The explorers gave it little thought as they went from room to room. They found nothing of interest until, in an upstairs linen closet, one of the boys noticed the wainscoting was loose. He gave a tug and the board came off. Behind it was an iron panel. When the panel was removed it led to a tunnel that dropped abruptly to a secret chamber where the ocean could be heard sloshing back and forth.

"It's where the ghost lives," suggested one of the boys. They ran from the room, clamored down the stairs and raced outside. Zina stopped them, "I left my handkerchief. I must go back." She dashed inside. A moment later a terrifying shriek followed by screams and moans tore apart the world.

"We're coming, Zina!" The students surged inside. They searched upstairs and found a pool of blood and Zina's handkerchief. And to their horror, the panel and the wainscoting had been replaced in the linen closet. They could not pry it loose.

Zina's body was never recovered. And the mystery ship still has not returned to the Oregon coast.

BLACK SILK KERCHIEF

"Every boy goes through a treasure hunting stage — he reads *Treasure Island* and starts dreaming about striking it rich. I was no different," said Orville Jones.

"When I was a kid one story that circulated through that part of the country was about a fellar who stole $20,000 in gold and buried it somewhere on the Cold Springs Ranch. He was lynched without telling where he buried it.

"My chum and I spent several Saturdays out on the ranch without unearthing a single clue. Then one afternoon I happened to notice a depression in the prairie. So we began digging. Maybe two feet down my shovel struck something that made the metal ring and I was sure I had struck the box in which the gold had been buried. I got down on my knees and went to work digging with my hands, scooping the dirt away.

"It was soon evident that my find was bone and a little more digging uncovered a man's skull with a bullet stuck in the bone. I shook the skull and the bullet fell out.

"We continued to dig and the next thing we struck was his arm bones, which were crossed at the wrist and tied together with this." He held up a black handkerchief. "Made out of silk. Silk doesn't rot.

"We dug out the whole skeleton, but there was no gold. We asked around but none of the oldtimers could offer any clue as to who we had found. So that was that.

"Ah, but if this black silk scarf could talk. What a tale it could tell...."

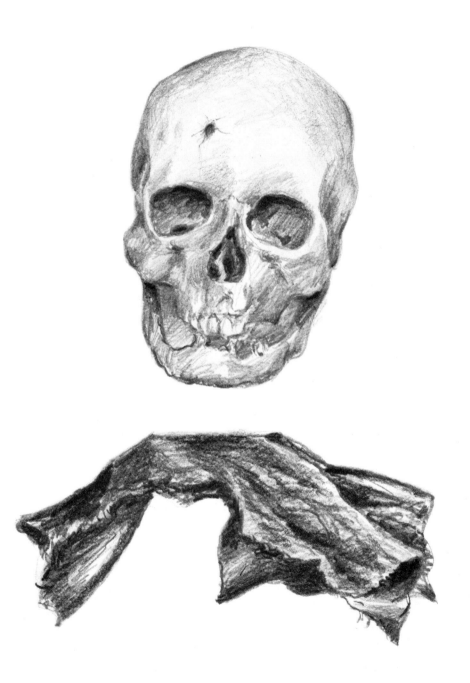

Rick Steber's Tales of the Wild West series is available in hardbound books ($12.50) and paperback books ($4.95) featuring illustrations by Don Gray, as well as in cassette tapes ($9.95) narrated by Dallas McKennon. A complete teacher study guide for the Tales of the Wild West series is also available ($8.95). Current titles in the series include:

❏ Vol. 1   Oregon Trail
❏ Vol. 2   *Pacific Coast*
❏ Vol. 3   *Indians*
❏ Vol. 4   *Cowboys*
❏ Vol. 5   *Women of the West*
❏ Vol. 6   *Children's Stories*
❏ Vol. 7   *Loggers*
❏ Vol. 8   *Mountain Men*
❏ Vol. 9   *Miners*
❏ Vol. 10   *Grandpa's Stories*
❏ Vol. 11   *Pioneers*
❏ Vol. 12   *Campfire Stories*

Bonanza Publishing
Box 204
Prineville, Oregon 97754